BROKEN MIRROR

A JOURNEY OF SELF-REFLECTION

CHEVERRO ANANSE SAVAGE

Broken Mirror:
A Journey of Self-Reflection

Copyright © 2025 Cheverro Ananse Savage

ISBN (Paperback): 979-8-89672-039-3
ISBN (Hardback): 979-8-89672-085-0
ISBN (Ebook): 979-8-89672-042-3

Printed in the United States of America.

PROMINENT
BOOKS

5830 E 2nd St, Ste 7000 #9983
Casper, WY 82609
USA

CONTENTS

For Charles Andrew Savage and Kenya

Jermaine Murray

May you two forever live in our hearts

PREFACE

The day my father passed, I remember it like it was yesterday. Valentine's Day 2007 and I had a date, a double date to be exact. A friend of mine had a perfect set up with live music, food and drinks. Just a place where you and your companion could relax, have a good time. I was looking forward to the outing because I was actually kind of new to the area and I didn't go out much. So in anticipation for the night, I just laid in my bed until it was time to get ready and release some stress.

My phone rings and as I go to reach for it, I noticed that on the screen, it had the words, "Dad" on it. I didn't bother to answer because I knew that he was going to lecture me on school, real estate or just something random that he saw on the news. Ten minutes go by and my phone rings again. I figured this would be one of my friends calling to cancel or something seeing as though it was still early. I look at the phone and it says, "Dad" again. He never calls twice I thought to myself. I answer the phone this time and it is my aunt.

She says, "Hey Che, how are you doing?" "I'm good, I replied.

Now I am laying down on my bed and I just can't
stop thinking, why is my aunt calling me on my dad's
phone to begin with? I start to feel awkward and
nervous. Things just didn't sit well with me.

"Why are you calling me on my dad's phone?" I asked her.

She doesn't reply right away and she stayed
silent for about ten seconds.

"You should call your uncle," she says.

Now, I had to take a deep breathe cause if it's one thing my
aunt likes to do and that's talk. All of a sudden she wants to pass
the phone to my uncle and he hates talking. This can't be good.

I hung up the phone with my aunt and before I called my
uncle I put the phone down to prepare myself. Honestly
I had no idea what to expect but I knew something was
off. My hands started shaking and I just didn't want
to make that call. So after minutes of deliberation, I
decided to call my uncle. After two rings, he answers.

"Hello?"

"Hey man, this is Che, Shirley told me to call you."

"Yea, ok, so how is everything." He asked.

"I'm cool man, just relaxing, nothing much." I replied.

"Cool, cool man, glad everything is good.

So.... your father passed away today, so, are you still in school and all that." "Whoa, hold up." I stopped him.

Did he just nonchalantly mention my father passed and go on to another topic? "Hey man, did you just say my father died?" I asked.

"Yea, he passed away today," He softly admitted.

"Man, let me call you back," I hang up the phone.

I am in disbelief at this point. I had a feeling that something bad may have happened, but death, no way. My father was healthy and ate his vegetables. I know he had his issues but he was a very responsible man. I stared at my phone for about twenty seconds, then I decide to call my mother. She answered the phone in three rings and says, "So you heard about your father?" "What?! You mean to tell me I was the last person to know. Damn!" "You already know son, I just found out myself," she continues to explain.

"Yea, they tried to reach you but no one had your number. So yea, you are the last to know."

I was blown away, I was young when I first experienced death but to lose a parent, I was devastated. I had to get off the phone and deal with my emotions.

CHEVERRO ANANSE SAVAGE

"Let me call you back," I said to my mother.

"Ok, no problem, take your time," she hangs up.

The only thing I could think of was to call my friend whom just lost his father a couple of months earlier. I call him, trying to hold back tears, he answers on 7 rings, I almost hung up.

"Hey what's up man", he answered. "Nothing much, I was calling because my father passed away and I wanted to know how you dealt with the passing of your father." I said quietly.

I felt bad for bringing up old memories because I remember the day his dad died and I brought flowers to his home.

He responded, "Man it was hard, I was angry, mad, upset and I was pissed at him, for leaving me. You learn to deal with the pain but it stays with you, always. Sorry for your loss man, I hope I was able to help." He said in a very sincere tone.

"Yea man, I appreciate it, thanks, I'll let you go, talk to you later." I replied back sobbing. Man, I didn't know what to think, then I remembered I had to cancel my double date. I called my boy first to let him know that I had to cancel. As I'm dialing his number, I just want to go into isolation and hide from the world. You think to yourself, "Why my father?"

It's crazy because I know it just happened to a
friend of mine and he felt the same exact way that
I am feeling now. Ken answers the phone.

"Hey man, what's up?" His voice is upbeat.

I felt bad that I had to cancel but there is no way that I
can go out in public feeling the way that I am feeling.

"My bad man, I have to cancel, I just got the news
that my dad died, so I won't be going anywhere
tonight." I said as I wiped tears from my eyes.

"It's cool man, you just take care of yourself, we
can go out anytime." He replied back.

Now, I have to do this again. I call Dianna to let her
know that I won't be able to go on the double date.

"Hello, hey, what's up, I'm actually getting ready right now,
what are you doing?" She says with an excited tone to her voice.

This sucks man. On Valentine's Day of all days, this day
will never be the same. I had to let her know the news.

"So look, I have to cancel, my dad just passed
so I have to deal with what's going on with me
right now." I told her breathing heavily.

"Oh, ok, sorry to hear that, do you think your friend
would still want to hang out?" She asked.

Boy was I in shock, she didn't give a damn about my
situation, just as long as she went out with some dude.

"I don't know, just call him." I said disappointed in her reaction. I gave her his number and hung up the phone. Low and behold Ken calls me two minutes after I hang up with Dianna.

"Hey man, your girl just called me asking if I still wanted to hang out." He said in despondent tone.

"It's cool man, you can still chill with her, I won't be offended." I replied.

"Man I told her I'm good, I'm not going out, I'm just going to stay in, you just stay strong man." He said as he hung up the phone.

As I laid there in my bed, laying on my back staring at the wall, all I could think of was my mom. The thought of losing her just made me cry even more. She has had high blood pressure her whole life and she is a couple years removed from heart surgery to correct a birth defect that caused her to have high blood pressure. I didn't expect to lose a parent. After my mother had her surgery, I just knew I had added time with both of them. My father's passing kind of came out of nowhere. He didn't seem to have any issues at all. Congenital heart failure was his cause of death and that had a lot to do with him having high blood pressure. Many of my family members have high blood pressure and all I can hope for is that they take their medication regularly because for all intents and purposes, my father did not.

A glass of wine sits on a coffee table while hot water is in a pan no longer boiling on the stove. The lights are on in the bathroom with all the toiletries prepped ready for use. Pacific is the atmosphere, very impassive in mood. Sounds of dripping water a distant memory. Worried faces begin to dial a number, the phone just rings, leaving more reason to check out the scene. A woman arrives at the door only to notice a car in a position that takes away any suspicions. Tranquil is the abode, soon to be a locality no longer referred to as, "Home." The domicile appears to be clear due to the scarcity of activity and the inadequacy to answer the knocks from the porch. She asks the manager for an extra set of keys, he opens the entrance and takes a step inside. Only to find a man undressed lying on a couch, motionless, breathless, and spiritless. The woman cannot go in to experience her brother's descent. This will bring forth feelings of nostalgia but we all are comforted by the fact that finally he is in harmony with the soil of his roots.

FATHER

Tears of a man flow so powerful, the emotion so deep it is hard not to lose control. Rising above our own depression an illusion is created but we remain transparent. Memories of a time when you were alive, keeps life unbalanced always trying to turn back the tide. Your voice never heard the magnitude of change, what is to be expected when your own mortality is in question? We cannot fear the future or try to exist in the past, surviving as a ghost will not last. A Photo album with pictures shows me as child, in the arms of my father smiling with pride.

Groundwork is key, must be laid to advance. A crack in the foundation can ruin a dam, we all know what happens when you can't place your feet in the sand. To access stability we all must be willing to lose some of our sanity. Sacrifices are made, actions we can't take back, words are misspoken many of which are not facts. We live in the moment, not five steps ahead, imagine if we did, everyone would know exactly what to expect. We learn from those who made us, they teach us, they love us. In a perfect world no one would leave, each kid born would be raised in a loving family. Success would be inherent, integrity encapsulated, stress annihilated. Hard work ingrained but the truth is much of who we are and all that we love can be gone in an instant, our life as we know it would have been in vain.

FROM A LOVING DAUGHTER

Strong in nature, a woman by design, my life is your life even though you created mine. Not a moment passes that you are not on my mind. In pictures we are identical, side by side. As I was young we were never close but our relationship grew. Thank you, for allowing me to know the man that I never knew. Inside I am crying and yet it remains silent. I stay strong for my daughters who miss their grandfather. My eyes are weary, my spirit is erupting, but the future ahead reminds me to stay focused. My life will go on as I watch my own babies grow, I know you will always be with me, you love me, I know.

Hidden in the abyss of our souls, only seen deep within our eyes, the truth they say, so we are told. To confront the notion that this is true, do we also believe the lies or do we seek the forbidden fruit? Peeling back what is on the surface only conceals another layer of uncertainty, whatever it is you search for won't be underneath what is culminating to be free. Death is imminent only if life is guaranteed, one of which you work hard at the other can come effortlessly. Dreams become goals which in turn is a legacy that takes shape once we reach and grab the gold. What are we to expect when our essence is eternal rest. All that is gained cannot come with us once we are placed in our grave but we give all we have to be memorialized in the sentience of our being for all those who do not know us can appreciate us unconditionally.

BEST KEPT SECRET

Secrets in the dark only heard by those who care, whispers in the night only told to those we cherish. No one knows the truth behind closed doors; everything is kept quiet and silent. Deep thoughts are always shared but it is up to you to realize what was said. A voice is never heard unless someone speaks; it is good when we listen so we can be able to find what we seek. Answers never lie in the questions we ask, there is always someone that knows what you lack. Persistence is the key to unlocking resistance; we have to go after what we want as if we need it. There is nothing we should fear except for ourselves because the best kept secret is that we are our own living hell.

Born in adulation but raised in chaos, the sparkle of the light always seen but those who truly witnessed seemed to miss what was foreseen. Dramatic irony of sorts, like someone reading a book, the audience knows the ending but the characters are lost. Some say fate is preordained, we can open our mind, like with magnetic pulses to the brain but our shortcomings win out as we self-sabotage our way out. We stroll our way into an existence that we are given, many an encumbrance but we hold dear to overcome it. The battle within, what is lost can be found, our truest attributes are our guide but do we truly care to walk the line? Question after question after question arise, how could we have prevented this, how could we have seen the signs? Letters engraved throughout the air that we breathe, nothing will be tangible, and we just have to believe. Self-doubt leads us to not trusting our intuition which is a mistake because it's there for a reason.

I REMEMBER

I remember your smile, I remember your laughter, and it is hard to believe you are in the here-after. I remember the pain the whole family went through, the day of your death, we all cried for you. I try so hard to see you in my dreams but for some reason, they always come up empty. Nights would not go by without a tear in my eye, then the sun would shine and it seemed that the day would just rewind. My mind was young, never knowing what really happened until I grew up. As adults we will never meet, just thoughts of "What if" or "What could have been." A lifetime of life without the ones you hold dear could be a lifetime of regret if you stop living the life that you have. Remember the past but understand that your presence is a gift, cherish the memories, never forget.

Screams never heard pierce the heart so hard, reaching
for a hero only to find the wrath of a mom. Too young to
understand but not too young to learn, trying to grasp the
concept of growing up in a broken home. The sound of flesh
against a fist was a familiar sound; a person can only withstand
so much before they break down. Mentally handicapped,
handcuffed from love's hand, who could persevere from such
an unpleasant reality to become a phenomenal woman. Fierce
in rage, unpredictable to this day, who could ever relate to such
a story that goes against the grain? Visually, the belief is the
antithesis of beauty. Hard to look at what is always beaten.
Determination wills the survivor even if that person was
lambasted for resembling their father. Time heals wounds
which sustain strength; adulthood has brought so less guilt.
Walking from the darkness into the light, love was waiting
and did not put up a fight. Refined in style, attractive to the
eye, who would have ever thought that day would arrive.
Independent, the sparkle has not dimmed, so enthusiastic
about the future because the world has given in. With the
ability to breathe, and now walking on solid concrete it is truly
refreshing, such a relief to smile in the essence of purity.

ANNA

Rooms are frozen, watch the walk, watch the strut, watch the movement of a being, your eyes are not being deceived. Jaws drop in awe of loveliness personified, confidence is magnetic, and humans gravitate to the symmetry, exquisite in imagery with a captivating personality. Eyes are seen in the shadows as they illuminate with a radiance that even the same sex can appreciate. Her capricious face leaves wonder and curiosity to where no man can breathe a breath of fresh air. Intimidated by this butterflies ambition, applauded in rhythm, nature has only one word for this marvel of a mortal, Anna.

Determination is dedication to the destruction of execration. The willingness to propel, the desire to excel, the intent to conquer, the commitment to delete all of which we don't need. What notion of belief that says, "Can't" is admirable when many of us believe it was coined to defeat us. Strength is in numbers so weakness is drawn from the sin of our skin. Toughness is taught, subside your anger and rage, to convince ourselves we can beat the burly oppressor we must be knowledgeable of our adversary. All points of contact, when to hit, when not to strike back, not every attack should end with blood but every battle does leave a bruise, scars and wounds. True test will find a way to destroy our ego, we can only envelop the demon to figure out a way to defeat the anti-hero. Nothing is without cause, we form bonds that sometimes break but we move on to mode another one.

STAND

The fierce competitive nature unleashes the true animalistic behavior in many of us. No longer the passive aggressive stance once taken, has a dignitary awakened? Forced out of containment, pushed to the brink, a man of few words is compelled to speak. Weakened by his tormentor, strength is established from within a man whom has just become a man now able to stand. Fist clinched, arms raised, he draws power from the heavens to relinquish the demons that once haunted his spirit. Embodied with confidence, vigor gained from perseverance, poised to challenge his adversaries as he rises from the ashes.

A tortured soul, from an infant to a toddler to a young
man to a grown man, astrology couldn't predict this type of
personality. A bad seed conceived on the eve of Halloween.
Innocence lost, unbeknownst to those close to him, as he
would age, the thin line between right and wrong became
blurred. Money, the root of all evil would be his downfall. A
person's environment normally influences behavior. Parents
are not involved, not loving enough and the streets become
the head of the household. Attraction to violence, the hustle,
women, guns and nice vehicles were too nice to overlook.
Even with a good foundation, from the outside looking in,
the illustration that the streets painted was just beautiful
and a sight to behold. The allure of hard work, education,
possibly raising a family was lost on him. No light to follow,
just darkness, the appeal of the night, the villainous role, able
to deceive, manipulate and be devoted to the ones he loved
seemed uncanny. Due to his duplicitous nature no one really
knew him, the person he really was but no one was surprised
to find out that he had the blood of virtue on his hands.

DJ

Intimidation in his voice, muscular physique, always ready to prove himself, even if he knew that he would face defeat. The thrill of the unknown, spontaneous to the bone, life on the edge, he walked a thin line, balancing act, as far as he was concerned, the Earth was flat. A juvenile delinquent, in the system before the age of fifteen, there was no rehabilitation, you can't tame a man who doesn't want to be tamed. The courts did their best to give him a chance, a job, housing and a mentor that turned his life around to now influence good behavior. His eyes saw a path, a road he wanted to choose, life, death or live without consequence. His choices made him the man whom he is today. A man who cannot walk freely, a man who cannot eat when and where he wants. A man who may never be with a woman again. A man, who is just a man, living as a man who may never live life on his terms and may die a man full of regret only to never live life as a grown man who chose a different path.

Lips move in unison to speak a universal language, heard
by those who miss the interpretation and to naïve to know
that they were chosen. We gravitate towards the glamor, the
charm it resonates, ignoring the possibility that it relocated
in our direction. Facial expressions can disguise the truth,
with a female it's internal and they can hide how they feel
in plain view. The glaring weakness in males lies within
not heeding the obvious, fearful of rejection so they remain
oblivious. Maturation can play a factor but there is no age that
is safe, wise men are even known to make mistakes. Our own
peculiar vacillation can leave us vulnerable in ways we can't
intuitively comprehend. Efforts to cultivate wealth is seen in
our culture as a way to become socially advantaged. Those
who are inept but gain acceptance through monetary means
are often seen as a false breed. Limits are only limits when we
limit ourselves, we all can be who we want others to see once
the paradigm shifts and we unapologetically show ourselves.

A WOMAN'S HEART

Fire and ice fuse in unison, an admirable presentation, similar to a sunset that boast a dazzling celebration. Dependable without fault, toughness unquestioned, authentic in their love and always willing to show affection. Mood can fluctuate depending on her station, if her infrastructure is cracking, be cautious because you will not like her when she's angry. Patience will be tested, fan the flames of the innocent, in this particular setting, there is no running to a secure location. Careful with the motion and be thoughtful of your companion, a woman can be handful but you should always remember to remain gentle.

The cycle will always continue, birth of a child, man and woman unite to embark on an adventure that eludes delineation. Pieces to a puzzle can sometimes be ambiguous but without those pieces the board is in disarray. History has shown we repeat our mistakes, only to show us how to be great. Each failure becomes an opportunity, every misstep a lesson, true character is often seen as forthrightness but many of us see it as a challenge to persuade. Gray areas never recognized, only scrutinized when the narrative is changed. Those who avoid confrontation are viewed upon as effete, as if the only way to prove man-hood is to be a combatant with a proven track record. Judgement is implanted on anyone with a pulse, even though we are educated not to judge anyone. The ability to adjust our perception and image is the greatest quality humanity conceived upon conception.

HUMAN

Purity is the sanctity of the essence of life.
Ageless figures of the imaginative mind never stop
to think about time. The creator of the creation
from the creative inhabitant that sought to express
their emotions through art, dance and song are
judged throughout history but never severely.
Research is needed to understand antiquities, resources
are needed to speak the language of the aborigine's. Born
in joy, true love and devotion, we are taught to hate,
fight, kill one another. Our breath is sacred, our minds
are invaluable and we must stop acting like kids who are
impressionable. Innocence lost in the wind, grown men
lost in sin. Before there was the need to survive there was
the will to stay alive. All has not been lost, we can find
our way back to the time we were not brainwashed.

In a state of flux, a rapid change in emotion can manifest as a disconnect with the opposite sex. Brace for impact, observing a chink in the armor has become elementary for those who can spot out a fraud with pin point accuracy. Everyone is a feature in their own epic fantasy, only the ending can end unpredictably. When summoned to a contest, will is tested, courage is revealed, or a lack thereof but what of a featherweight whose primordial instinct is to back away? Attitude can sway the circumstance but that's a chance not many are willing to yield. Surroundings and being aware of the situation can only advance in proper form if and when the participant plays confident in their role to conform. Many are not prepared to cease control but there always comes a time where you have to let go. Having faith in others grows with time and being able to allow yourself to shine is the gateway to finding what's been hidden in the wake of all that has already been designed.

LIFE IN THE BALANCE

Blessings upon us for each day we breathe, once you question reality, the door opens for you to leave. The thread so thin, barely visible to the eye, somehow we know it's there because we consistently question life. The love, hate relationship feels like a motion picture for the entire world to see, ultimately we all feel the same and we all have one life to lead. Smiles are contagious, so let's infect our mothers, fathers, sons, daughters and brothers. A generation of stainlessness, each being of clear conscience, marching with no agenda, a flawless execution of allegiance to one another. A basic civilized camaraderie where mortals are shoulder to shoulder with no evil sentiment, just a sound mind of natural affinity and each spirit looking forward to the future.

The division of man, what separates us is the environment of the land. Languages, accents, melanin and the intervals of Mother Nature all play a segment to all of the inhabitants. Characters wait their turn, even though everyone has a supporting role. Interactions are not scripted but sometimes they may feel contrived, no way was this all constructed but it comes off like it is sometimes. What's painless to some can be the death of a life force, impossible to figure out how one is immune but another with the same make up is doomed. Cautionary tale, usually too late, the ship has already sailed. Conditioned for survival within the laws of nature, pro-creation is a fundamental flaw because we do it for pleasure. Alliances taken for granted will depreciate our value, it is only when we grip what we appreciate close to our chest that awaken us and we are able to differentiate day from night.

MIRROR

Shards of broken glass scattered across the bedroom floor, bloody footprints leave traces of the remains, seven years of bad luck they say. The reflection painful to welcome, born into this world hating your face. Every feature would be erased, complexion totally changed, a new person would arrive just because of the dislike to what is inside. Origin story dismissed due to the stress their DNA caused, ancestors are at fault. Long road travelled but many do not hold dear the pain suffered from our ascendants to even care. What's on the surface can be replaced but no one can hide who they truly are even if they want to keep it hidden underneath. It is time to ascend above the trivial and look beyond what is now a spectacle, to truly become what we all are, which is beautiful.

ABOUT THE AUTHOR

Cheverro Ananse Savage is a freelance writer and poet. He is a member of the Alameda Writers Group. He is currently working on his latest project, a collection of short story/poetry reflecting on his times as an adolescent, transitioning from a young naive boy to a man.

AUTHOR SOCIAL MEDIA LINKS:

Twitter: @Cheverro @Anansepoetry

Facebook: Cheverro Ananse Savage

www.ingramcontent.com/pod-product-compliance
Lightning Source LLC
Chambersburg PA
CBHW051251120626
46547CB00014B/1897